INTERACTIVE OBJECT LESSONS
TRUSTING GOD

**by Joette Whims
and
Melody Hunskor**

STANDARD
PUBLISHING
Cincinnati, Ohio

The Standard Publishing Company, Cincinnati, Ohio
A division of Standex International Corporation

CONTENTS

INTRODUCTION

As children's leaders, we have in our hands the most exciting book in the world—the Bible. In it we find the most effective teacher of all time—Jesus Christ. He used unique methods of teaching that helped his listeners learn for themselves.

What would it have been like to be in the crowd of 5,000 when Jesus fed everyone with just five loaves and two fish? No one would need to tell you that Jesus could provide all your physical needs! Or, if you had been one of the disciples in the boat when Jesus calmed the sea and the wind, you would have understood immediately that Jesus could protect you.

As a teacher, Jesus used different methods of teaching. For example, the parables are stories that revolve around simple objects, such as coins, sheep, seeds, and trees—all things common to Jesus' listeners.

That's what this book will do for your students. You'll be able to present biblical principles through objects your kids can touch, see, smell, hear, and taste. As your students become actively involved in the lesson, they will grasp the point for themselves. They will get excited about discovering what God has to say to them.

This book is planned around some of the most common topics for children. The lessons are simple to prepare with objects you have around your home. They can be easily used with groups that contain multiple age levels. Use these lessons to supplement your teaching or as lessons by themselves. (Please note that all "teacher talk" is printed in **boldface** type to guide you in talking to your students.)

Kids are used to active learning methods in their school classrooms. Bring the excitement of sensory learning to your children's program at church too. Use as much or as little of the lesson as you want. The time needed for each lesson will vary depending on your students' needs, maturity, and interest, as well as the amount of time you have available in your schedule.

To extend the lesson, you may incorporate the take-home paper into your teaching time. The take-home paper is designed to inform parents of the topic studied and a biblical application. It also suggests a fun activity to reinforce the learning objective.

To shorten the lesson, demonstrate the lesson activity yourself; then engage the students in the discussion time. Either way, you will touch the curiosity of your audience as you actively engage your students in learning. And you'll enjoy learning biblical principles along with your kids!

1
HONEY, HONEY, HONEY

PSALM 119:103

BIBLE VERSE | "How sweet are your words to my taste, sweeter than honey to my mouth!" (Psalm 119:103).

OBJECTIVE | The students will learn that we can trust God's words which are sweet as honey.

MATERIALS | Bible, 3 different kinds of honey, plastic spoons, plastic knives, crackers, napkins, pencils, wax paper, paper bees

BEFORE CLASS | Before class, go to a grocery store or health food store and purchase three different kinds of honey. Some kinds you can buy are:

Clover honey: This is one of the most common types of honey. Farmers use the bees to pollinate the clover. The honey is mild and light.

Buckwheat honey: This is a dark honey with a strong, robust taste. It is made by bees who work in a buckwheat field.

Wildflower honey: This is made by bees in the wild who drink from wildflowers.

Orange honey: This is made by bees who pollinate orange blossoms.

Desert honey: This is made by bees who pollinate desert plants. It has a very distinctive taste.

Put the jars of honey on wax paper with a spoon in each jar.

7

This will help avoid a sticky cleanup. Provide a paper bee for each student. The bees can be made using the art on the take-home paper or purchased and added to squares of construction paper.

When students arrive, ask them to sit in a circle.

How many of you have ever seen bees at work? Describe some things you have seen them do.

(They fly from flower to flower. They go in and out of their hives. They chase people or animals away from their hives.)

When you watched bees doing these things, what were they busy making?

(Honey.)

Most people have tasted honey. But did you know that there are different kinds of honey? The flavor depends on the kind of flower the bee drinks from.

Today we are going to taste three different kinds of honey. Notice the difference in taste. Decide which one you like best. I am going to give you a paper bee. When you are finished tasting, set your bee beside the honey you like best.

Give each child three crackers, a plastic knife, a napkin, and a paper bee. Have kids put honey on their crackers one at a time so they can taste all the honey.

What did the honey taste like to you?

(Hold up the honey jars one at a time and have the students describe the taste. Some things they might say are *sweet, bitter, bad, good, funny, like an orange*.)

Then look at the number of paper bees beside each jar and determine the winner.

I'm sure most of us liked this honey because it was the sweetest. Did you know that the Bible talks about honey? In Psalm 119:103, it says, "How sweet are your words to my taste, sweeter than honey to my mouth!"

Why do you think the Bible says reading God's Word is like eating honey? Explain your answer.

(It makes us do sweet things and says God loves us.)

God's Word is sweet like honey because it helps us do what's right. In Psalm 19, verses 7 and 10, we read, "The law of the Lord is perfect, reviving the soul . . . sweeter than honey, than honey from the comb." When we spend time in God's Word every day, what we say and do will be like honey to people around us.

We all like it when people say nice things about us. The Bible says hearing pleasant words is like honey, too.

Read Proverbs 16:24.

How does it make you feel when someone says nice things about you?

(Really good, like I'm important.)

Think of one time when someone said something nice about you. What was it?

(My mom told me I have beautiful hair. My teacher said I had the best science project in class.)

Think of a time when you said something especially nice to someone else. What was it?

(I told my dad that he was a good driver. I told my friend that I like playing with her because she always shares her toys.)

Let's practice giving this kind of honey to each other. Turn to your neighbor on each side and say something nice to both of them. You can compliment them for the nice way they act or the things they can do well.

Give kids a few moments to compliment each other. Then take your turn saying nice things about each person in class. Then let volunteers share what others said about them.

Close with a prayer similar to this one:

Dear heavenly Father, thank you for your Word. Thank you that it teaches us, keeps us from doing what's wrong, and comforts us. Thank you also for the pleasant words that others say to us. In Jesus' name, amen.

Honey, Honey, Honey

BIBLE VERSE:
"How sweet are your words to my taste, sweeter than honey to my mouth!" (Psalm 119:103).

PARENTS:
Today your child learned that he or she can trust God's Word which is sweet like honey. The students tasted three different kinds of honey and decided which one they liked the best. We then read in the Bible that God compares his Word to honey. We also found out that God's Word helps to show us where to go and what to do, makes us wise, and keeps us from doing wrong. We realized we needed to be reading God's Word every day.

BUZZING TO READ MY BIBLE:
Cut out the bees on this page and let each bee represent a single family member. Daily have the bees go from flower to flower each time a family member has a personal quiet time with God. During this quiet time, each family member needs to read the Bible and pray. (For those younger children who cannot read, read to them.) When all the bees get to the hive, make the following honey snacks or provide any other honey treats you choose:

While enjoying the snack, talk about some of the things you learned by reading your Bibles this week. Discuss how God's Word is like honey.

Honey Bars
1 cup of honey
12 ounces of butterscotch chips
12 ounces of chocolate chips
6 cups of rice crisp cereal
1/2 cup of chopped nuts

Heat honey in a medium saucepan. Add the chips. Stir until melted. Pour over cereal and nuts. Mix well. Put into a buttered cake pan. When cool, cut into squares.

Nutty Bar Sticks
1 tablespoon of honey
1/2 cup of creamy peanut butter
chocolate chips or chopped peanuts
6 celery sticks

Cream the honey and peanut butter together. Fill celery sticks with mixture. Top with chopped peanuts or chocolate chips.

2 GINGERBREAD CREATIONS

MATTHEW 4:4

BIBLE VERSE

"It is written: 'Man does not live on bread alone, but on every word that comes from the mouth of God'" (Matthew 4:4).

OBJECTIVE

The students will learn that God's Word is nourishing bread to our spiritual lives.

MATERIALS

Bible, undecorated gingerbread cookies, icing of different colors, cake decorating beads and sprinkles, raisins, aluminum foil, red licorice laces, cinnamon candies, mixing bowls for icing, spreading utensils, paper, pencils
To conduct this lesson, you may either purchase undecorated gingerbread cookies or make them in class. Here is a recipe you can use:

Gingerbread Boys
1/2 cup butter or margarine
1/2 cup brown sugar
1/2 cup molasses
1 egg
1 1/2 teaspoons soda
1/2 teaspoon salt
1/2 teaspoon ginger
1 teaspoon cinnamon
2 1/2 cups flour
Cream butter, sugar, molasses, and egg. Sift dry ingredients together and add to creamed mixture. Mix well. Divide dough

into three parts. On a pastry cloth, roll out part of the dough. Cut cookies with a cutter and place on a lightly greased cookie sheet. Decorate with raisins, cinnamon candies, and licorice laces. Bake at 350° for 8-10 minutes until edges are brown. Loosen from cookie sheet before cookies cool completely.

If you plan to bake cookies in class:
Allow 30 extra minutes for your lesson. Gather the needed items for the recipe, which include margarine, brown sugar, molasses, eggs, soda, salt, ginger, cinnamon, flour, pastry cloth, rolling pin, mixing bowl, and utensils. Depending on how much time you have to spend on your lesson, you may either mix the dough in class, bring cooled dough to class, or cut out the cookies ahead of time and bring them to class. Hold your class in a roomy kitchen area. Have plenty of paper towels and hand soap available.

Let each student decorate his or her own cookie. Add raisins, cinnamon candies, and licorice laces before baking. Decorate with icing and sprinkles after cookies have cooled.

Present the lesson while the cookies are baking. Have an adult helper take hot pans in and out of the oven and put cookies on a cooling rack while you teach. When you finish, decorate the cooled cookies and have the students help you clean up the mess.

If you plan to purchase cookies:
Cover areas of your table with tinfoil. Make sure you have plenty of paper towels and a place for the students to wash their hands. When students arrive, decorate the cookies with beads, sprinkles, candies, and icing. Then set the creations on tinfoil to dry. Have the students help you clean up the mess and then sit in a semicircle.

What did you like best about the gingerbread creation you decorated?

(I put a licorice frown on his face. My cookie has pink cheeks and green hair.)

Gingerbread cookies are an old-time favorite. I'm sure many of your grandmothers made these cookies when they were young. Something that we eat that's even older than cookies is bread. People have been making bread for thousands of

years. Cookies and bread are made from grain. So are donuts, rolls, buns, macaroni, rice, and cereals. All these foods have lots of grain in them. Some types of grain are wheat, oats, and rice.

What kinds of bread do you eat at home?

The Bible talks about bread. Let's read what Jesus said about it.

Distribute Bibles. Pair readers with nonreaders. Have a volunteer read Matthew 4:4 while the other students follow along. Then have students turn back to Deuteronomy 8:3 to show them how the same verse is also found in the Old Testament.

How is eating bread like reading God's Word?

(Eating bread tastes good and reading the Bible feels good. We eat bread to stay healthy. We read God's Word to stay healthy in our spirits.)

The people who lived during the time Jesus lived on the earth relied on bread as a main food. They didn't have refrigerators or freezers to keep meat fresh. They didn't have plastic wrap or sandwich bags for storing vegetables and fruit. But they did know how to bake bread so it would last a long time. That's one reason why bread was so important to them.

How important is bread to us?

(Not as important. My family eats bread at every meal.)

What's an example of a meal you often eat at home?

(Allow students to give examples. As they do, point out the foods that have grain in them.)

Think of some things that wouldn't taste good without bread or other foods that have grain in them. What are they?

(Hamburgers, spaghetti, pizza.)

We wouldn't be very healthy without bread. We wouldn't be very healthy spiritually without God's Word. Let's see why.

Help kids select a partner. Give each pair a piece of paper and a pencil.

Together with your partner, write down things that might happen to a Christian who doesn't read his or her Bible for a long time.

Give kids two or three minutes to write. Circulate among the pairs to give suggestions to students who are having trouble coming up with ideas. Some suggestions are: They might forget God's rules. They will sin more. They will forget about how much God loves them.

When time is up, have kids reform the semicircle. Have each pair share their answers with the class.

How is knowing God's Word like eating bread?

(It goes inside you and becomes a part of you.)

What happens if you read or memorize God's Word but don't do what it says?

(It doesn't become a part of you. It doesn't do you any good.)

I like to think that God's Word is a little like our gingerbread creations. God's Word isn't plain or ordinary. Neither are our gingerbread creations. God's Word is beautiful. So are our creations.

But even more, God's Word doesn't just give our spirits energy like cookies do. God's Word changes us into loving, kind, patient people. It changes us from the inside out. We sparkle all over with God's love.

Right now, let's thank God for his delicious, spiritually nutritious Word to us. Let's begin by thanking him for the Bible story we like best.

Give kids a moment to think of a favorite Bible story. Then have volunteers thank God for their Bible story.

Now let's do something more difficult. Let's thank God for a rule in his Word that is hard to follow.

Begin by thanking God for a rule you find hard to follow. Then allow students to do the same. If kids have a hard time thinking of rules, remind them of the Ten Commandments. Conclude by thanking God for his supernatural Word which keeps us spiritually healthy.

Before you dismiss the students, either wrap their gingerbread creations in aluminum foil so they can take them home or enjoy a gingerbread snack together.

SANDWICH SHAPE-UPS

BIBLE VERSE:

"It is written: 'Man does not live on bread alone, but on every word that comes from the mouth of God'" (Matthew 4:4).

PARENTS:

Today your child learned that the Word of God is as important to our spiritual health as bread is to our physical health. Our class decorated gingerbread cookies and discussed how wonderful God's Word is when we obey it.

COOK'S NIGHT OUT:

For an evening meal this week, plan a fun activity—make Sandwich Shape-Ups.

Lay pieces of sliced bread on plastic wrap. Using large cookie cutters in shapes of stars, hearts, circles, etc., cut out those shapes from the bread. Make sure you cut an even number of pieces of each shape—two stars, four hearts, etc.

Make sandwiches from the bread shapes. You could use peanut butter and jelly, meat slices and cheese, or other family favorites. If you use meat slices and cheese, use your cookie cutters to make meat and cheese slices the same shape as the bread.

Arrange the sandwiches on a platter. Serve with a favorite salad dish.

When you finish eating, discuss how important God's Word is to your family. Then have each person read or recite his or her favorite Bible verse. Conclude with prayers of thanksgiving for the Bible.

Do not discard bread scraps. Instead, thread them on string and tie them to trees for bird food. You may even want to spread a little peanut butter on the larger scraps for the birds' gourmet delight!

3
FRUIT FACES

GALATIANS 5:22, 23

BIBLE VERSE

"The fruit of the Spirit is love, joy, peace, patience, kindness, goodness, faithfulness, gentleness and self-control. Against such things there is no law" (Galatians 5:22, 23).

OBJECTIVE

The students will learn the fruits of the Spirit and how to apply them to their lives.

MATERIALS

Bible, nine kinds of fruit, lemon juice, toothpicks, table knives, white icing, trays, paper, pencils, paper towels

BEFORE CLASS

Before class, select nine kinds of fruit to represent the nine fruits of the Spirit. Since the students will be making fruit people, pick some fruits that can be used later as decorations, such as pineapple chunks or raisins. Leave other fruits whole to use as faces, such as apples or oranges. Examples of what you could bring are given for you but feel free to substitute your choices. If necessary you could also use vegetables, such as carrot slices or peas. Sprinkle apples and bananas with lemon juice to keep them from turning brown. Prepare and label each fruit with its corresponding fruit of the Spirit.

Examples:
Love—whole apples
Joy—whole orange or orange section
Peace—pineapple chunks
Patience—raisins

16

Kindness—small strawberries or strawberry slices
Goodness—banana slices
Faithfulness—grapes
Gentleness—blueberries
Self-control—cherries

Have your kids wash their hands before this activity. Then form groups of four. Give each group a Bible, tray, toothpicks, table knife, icing, paper, and pencil. Set out paper towels. Have each group assign a recorder.

The Bible talks about kinds of fruit that Christians should have in their lives. In your group, read Galatians 5:22, 23 and have your recorder write down each kind of fruit mentioned in the verses.

Give students a few minutes to write down the fruits.

Today, we're going to make fruit people. I've matched each kind of fruit on the table with a fruit of the Spirit. Your group will make a person using at least seven of the nine kinds of fruit. To do that, you must buy fruit from me. To buy a piece of fruit, you must tell me one way you can show its fruit of the Spirit in your life.

For example, your group may decide to buy an apple for the face. The apple matches love. First discuss one way you could show love to someone and have the recorder write it on your piece of paper. You might write, "I can show love by sharing my snack with my brother." Or "We show love when we let someone else have the first turn on the school computer." Then tell me what you wrote. You must do this for each piece of fruit you want to buy. Make your fruit person on the tray using the icing and toothpicks to stick the parts together. You may start now.

As groups work, give suggestions on what to say for "fruit actions."

When groups finish, gather in a circle. Have each group show the fruit person they made. Have each recorder tell several ways the group thought of to show the fruits of the Spirit.

Why is it so important to do the fruits of the Spirit?

(Because God wants us to, and we can do what's right.)

17

How does God help us have the fruits of the Spirit?

(He gives us the Holy Spirit. He tells us what to do in the Bible.)

Why do you think love is the most important fruit?

(If you have love, you'll do the rest of the fruits of the Spirit.)

Have a volunteer read 1 Corinthians 13:4-7.

God uses his power to help us practice the fruits of the Spirit. We can't do them on our own. But when we ask God every day to let his fruit grow in our lives, he helps us show love, joy, peace and all the rest.

Let's ask God to give us his fruit this week. Think of one fruit you will probably need this week. Maybe you have a hard science test coming up and need self-control to study hard. Or maybe you have trouble getting along with someone who sits near you in your classroom and you need to show more love. I'll pray first. When I pause, silently ask God to give you the one fruit of the Spirit for the situation you thought of.

Pause to let students think, then pray:

Dear Jesus, thank you for your Spirit who helps us grow godly fruit in our lives. Thank you that your power is greater than any situation we face. Please help us show your fruit in our lives this week in the situations we thought of. Pause to give students time to pray silently. Help us have more of your fruit every day. Amen.

Encourage the kids to share their fruit people creations with each other as you enjoy the snack.

FRUIT FACES

BIBLE VERSE:

"The fruit of the Spirit is love, joy, peace, patience, kindness, goodness, faithfulness, gentleness and self-control. Against such things there is no law" (Galatians 5:22, 23).

PARENTS:

Today in class, your child learned about the fruits of the Spirit and how to apply them in his or her life. Our class did this by making fruit people. We assigned each kind of fruit a characteristic, such as joy or peace. As groups used each piece of fruit, they gave one example of how to show that fruit of the Spirit in their lives.

FAMILY FUN:

Place a small basket somewhere handy to all family members. Set the fruit drawings and scissors near the basket. When someone displays the characteristic of a piece of fruit, cut it out and place it in the basket. When all of the fruit is in the basket, have a fruit sundae as a family and discuss each fruit of the Spirit and its actions. The following are some examples of each fruit that you may choose to do:

Love: Write a letter to grandparents telling them how much they mean to you.
Joy: Thank Jesus for the hard things in your life. Sing instead of getting mad.
Peace: Walk away from a fight. Don't argue with your brother.
Kindness: At school, eat lunch with someone who usually eats alone. Compliment someone in your family.
    Goodness: Say something good about a person your friends are gossiping about. Pick up your baby sister's toys without being asked.

Patience: Try to work that hard math problem a third time. Keep your room clean for a whole week.
Gentleness: Help a little kid who has gotten hurt. Talk softly when someone is shouting at you.
Faithfulness: Read your Bible every day for a week. Take out the trash without being reminded.
Self-Control: Do your homework instead of playing video games. Keep your temper in check when someone calls you a name.

4
GROWING UP HEALTHY

1 PETER 2:2

BIBLE VERSE

"Like newborn babies, crave pure spiritual milk, so that by it you may grow up in your salvation" (1 Peter 2:2).

OBJECTIVE

The students will learn how God's Word makes all of a Christian's life better.

MATERIALS

Bibles, powdered chocolate milk, toast, cereal, instant pudding, butter, milk, plates, bowls, glasses, spoons, paper, pencil, paper towels

Ahead of time, write all these references on a piece of paper: Psalm 119:98; Psalm 119:99; Psalm 119:100; Psalm 119:101. Make enough copies so each student can have one.

BEFORE CLASS

Set out plates, small bowls, glasses, and spoons. As students come in, tell them that you are going to have a delicious snack. Ask the kids to find a place at the table. Take a piece of paper and get their orders for the snack. They may choose: chocolate milk, cereal, toast, and/or pudding.

After taking orders, serve powdered chocolate milk, toast without butter, dry cereal, and powdered pudding. Do not add milk or butter to any of these items. Make each serving approximately a one-serving amount.

Please don't eat any of your food until after we have thanked God for it.

What's wrong with our snacks?

(The food isn't made. Everything looks funny.)
Pray for the food, then allow students to taste their food.

Please don't eat more than a taste because we're going to do something with the snacks later. Just for now, let's set our snacks aside. Let's make a semicircle here on the floor.

Have students form a semicircle in an area apart from the table so no one will be distracted by the food. Distribute Bibles. Form pairs. Make sure nonreaders are paired with readers.

Our snacks were missing something important—milk. With your partner, think of foods you like that have milk in them. Let me give you one clue. Butter and cream come from milk so they are also milk products. You may also list foods that contain butter or cream.

Give kids a couple of minutes to think of foods with milk in them. Then form the semicircle with partners sitting next to each other.

I'm going to ask each pair to stand and give their list, one food at a time. If you like the food they mention, stand up. If you don't like that food, stay seated.

Have each pair stand and slowly share their list.

What was the most popular milk food?

(Ice cream, cheese.)

Milk is such an important part of our meals. It is the only thing that babies eat or drink. Without milk, they couldn't live.
  God says that his Word, the Bible, is like milk.

Have partners read 1 Peter 2:2 to each other.

How does milk help our bodies grow?

(It makes our bones strong. It gives us vitamins and energy.)

When newborn babies want milk, how do they act?

(They cry and wiggle all over.)

The apostle Peter gives us a good example of how the Bible is like milk. He says milk is pure and makes us grow strong.

21

He says we should love the Bible like newborn babies love their milk.

Newborn babies have huge appetites. They want to eat all the time. They get impatient when they don't get their milk. They want their milk now! When they drink pure milk, they grow and grow.

Distribute the pieces of paper with the references on them.

God's Word makes every part of our lives better, just like milk does for a baby. Look up these verses. For each, write one way that God's Word makes our lives better and helps us grow up healthy in our spirits.

Give students about three or four minutes to write.

What are the ways you found that God's Word makes our lives better?

(We get wiser than our enemies. We can stay away from evil.)

Without saying anything mean about anyone else or speaking in a boastful way, can you think of an example where one of these answers is true in your life?

Depending on the age of your students, they may need help responding to this question.

Now, let's enjoy our snacks! Let me explain how we'll make our food better. One-by-one, we'll add milk or butter. As you add the milk product, tell one way that God's Word keeps you strong and helps you grow spiritually.

Have kids sit at their same places. Bring out cold milk and butter. As you help each person add milk or butter to each food, have him or her tell one way God's Word makes him or her strong and healthy. It's okay if kids repeat what their neighbor says.

Then thank God for the food and for his pure Word. Enjoy the snacks! When finished, have kids help you clean up the mess before they leave.

GROWING UP HEALTHY

BIBLE VERSE:

"Like newborn babies, crave pure spiritual milk, so that by it you may grow up in your salvation" (1 Peter 2:2).

PARENTS:

Today your child learned about how important God's Word is for spiritual growth. We studied how the Bible is like pure milk. The class had a snack of chocolate milk, toast, cereal, and pudding. As we added milk or butter to each food, we described ways the Bible acts like pure milk to make us strong and healthy in our spirits. Then we thanked God for his Word.

Make a spiritual growth chart for each person in your family. The chart could look like this:

After one week, have a growth check to see how much each person stretched his or her spiritual muscles. Try it for another week and compare growth again. Then serve ice cream sundaes to celebrate your diet of learning God's Word.

HOW TO GROW

I read my Bible today. *(Add two inches.)*

I practiced what I read in my Bible today. *(Add three inches.)*

I memorized a verse today. *(Add five inches!)*

Stretch Your Spiritual Muscles

Giant-size
Over 7' tall!

7'

6'

5'

Good going.
Great growth!

4'

3'

2'

Newborn 20"
Start here

5
FOLLOW THE LEADER

JOHN 10:27

BIBLE VERSE

"My sheep listen to my voice; I know them, and they follow me" (John 10:27).

OBJECTIVE

The students will see that if you follow someone, you need to listen to and obey that person. That's the way we follow Jesus.

MATERIALS

Bible, masking tape, pencils, paper, and items to make an obstacle course such as chairs, string, large blocks from the nursery department, medium size boxes, or small rugs

BEFORE CLASS

Before class, tape two parallel lines on the floor where you'll build an obstacle course.

When students arrive, form groups of four. Pass out a piece of paper and pencil to each group. Have each group think of one reason that may keep a person from following Jesus. Some examples are: thinking about money, wanting your own way, pride, getting too busy, or forgetting to read your Bible. Instruct each group to write the reason in large letters on their piece of paper.

Display the items to build an obstacle course. Have each group select what they need to make one obstacle in the course. Some suggestions for obstacles are: two chairs set apart with string tied between the legs so the follower has to step over it, blocks stacked so closely on two sides that the follower has to walk toe-to-heel to get through, small rugs placed as stepping stones, boxes set one step apart like hurdles. Guide the groups so they don't make the obstacle impossible to go over. Then have groups tape their reason on their part of the course.

Invite two volunteers to be the first to go through the course. Appoint one the follower and the other the leader. Give these rules:

The follower must walk with a pencil balanced on the back of his or her closed fists. If the pencil is dropped, the follower must go back to the start.

This obstacle course is like our lives. We have many obstacles to overcome. Here are some of them.

(Read the reasons taped to the obstacles).

The Bible says that when we follow Jesus, he helps us through the obstacles in life. Jesus says, "My sheep listen to my voice; I know them, and they follow me." But sometimes we forget to follow Jesus. Then we have trouble getting over the obstacles in our lives. Let's see what it's like to go through our obstacle course alone.

First, have the follower go through the obstacle course alone. Each group should cheer for the follower to get over their obstacle when he or she gets to it. For example, if the group named their obstacle "thinking too much about money," the kids in the group could cheer by saying, "Money isn't as important as Jesus!" or "Don't think about money, think about Jesus!"

The follower will find that it's almost impossible to make it through the obstacle course without dropping the pencil because he or she can't concentrate fully on balancing the pencil and getting through the obstacles at the same time. If the follower does drop the pencil, he or she must go back to the starting point.

Now let's have the same follower go through the obstacle course with the leader's help. Follower, you keep your eyes on the pencil and listen to the directions the leader gives. Leader, if the pencil drops, you may pick it up and put it back on the follower's hand.

Have the leader help the follower go through the course. As long as the follower keeps his or her eyes on the pencil and follows directions carefully, the follower can make it through the obstacle course. The leader can also replace the pencil on the follower's hand if it is dropped. Have groups cheer when the follower goes through their part of the course.

Have the other pairs try the obstacle course.
After they finish the course, gather kids in a circle.

Why was it so hard for the follower to get through the obstacle course by himself or herself?

(She couldn't concentrate on two things at once. The pencil wouldn't stay on his hand.)

How is this like trying to go through life without Jesus' help?

(We can't make it without Jesus' help when we run into trouble.)

What was different about the second time the follower went through the obstacle course?

(She had help. Someone could tell him what to do.)

Followers, how did having a leader help you?

(I could listen to directions. It felt nice to have someone help me.)

How important is it to have a good leader to follow? Why?

(Important because otherwise we would get lost. Important because we can't do everything by ourselves.)

How is Jesus a good leader?

(He always stays by our side. He knows more than people do.)

What happened when the follower didn't listen to the leader?

(He couldn't get through the obstacles and kept dropping the pencil.)

How is that like what happens when we forget to listen to Jesus?

(We might get into trouble and not know how to get out. We can't figure out how to get around the things that bug us.)

Jesus is the best leader to follow. Let's thank him for being our leader. Think of one way Jesus helps you in your life.

Pray sentence prayers, letting volunteers thank Jesus for being their leader.

FOLLOW THE LEADER

START

Help Mom without being asked.

Do homework without being told.

Read the Bible today.

Make my bed in the morning.

Get ready for bed on time.

Pray for 2 minutes.

BIBLE VERSE:

"My sheep listen to my voice; I know them, and they follow me" (John 10:27).

PARENTS:

Today in class, your child learned about following a leader. He or she learned that we need to listen to and obey our leaders. This is one way to follow Jesus. This was illustrated by following a leader through an obstacle course. Your child had to follow a leader with a pencil balanced on the back of his or her closed fists. This obstacle course was compared to his or her life.

FAMILY FUN:

Hang this game board on your refrigerator or somewhere handy. Make a marker for each child in the family. Discuss how parents are the leaders in the family. Discuss how God commands children to obey parents. By obeying parents they are following Jesus. Jesus also is our example and did many of the things on this game board. Have each child flip a coin. If he or she gets heads, he or she moves two spaces. If tails, he or she moves one. The player must do the directions on each square before flipping the coin to move on. When everyone in the family makes it to the finish line, hold a Family Fun Obstacle Course Night. Set up a small obstacle course in your yard or recreation room. You can have your children crawl under chairs, step on rugs, step over rope, crawl through hula hoops, dribble balls, etc. When finished, pop popcorn and discuss some of the following questions:

Why is it hard to follow a leader?
What was the hardest thing for you to do on the game board and why?
What are some things that Jesus did that we should follow as our leader?
What are some ways you can follow Mom and Dad as leaders?

FINISH

Give somebody a surprise.

Take over a chore for my brother or sister for a day.

Be a friend to someone who is lonely.

Compliment somebody.

Read a Christian book.

Set the table for supper. | Pray for someone I don't like. | Clean my room without being reminded. | Do yard work. | Invite someone to church. | Tell a Bible story to someone.

6 BRIDGE OVER RAGING WATERS

MATTHEW 7:13, 14; JOHN 14:6

BIBLE VERSE

"Enter through the narrow gate. . . . But small is the gate and narrow the road that leads to life, and only a few find it" (Matthew 7:13, 14). "Jesus answered, 'I am the way and the truth and the life. No one comes to the father except through me'" (John 14:6).

OBJECTIVE

The students will learn that trusting Jesus is the only bridge to God.

MATERIALS

Bible, paper plates, straws, cups, newspapers, tape, glue, three or four hardcover books equal in size, pencils, construction paper, and poster board or cardboard

BEFORE CLASS

Before class, put the paper plates, straws, cups, newspapers, tape, and glue in easily accessible piles for students to use. Cut crosses out of sturdy construction paper or poster board. Make one for each child. If possible, find pictures of different bridges.

When students arrive, have them sit in a circle. Hold up a picture of a bridge.

**This is a picture of a bridge. A bridge has several uses.
Think about some of the bridges you have crossed.
What were those bridges used for?**

(Have students give answers. Include most of the following: *to get across a body of water, to go over railroad tracks, to get from one high hill to another, to get across a road or freeway.)*

If you cut out pictures of bridges, show them as each type is mentioned. Then have the students form groups of 3 or 4.

Today we're going to build our own bridges. I have several things you can use: paper plates, newspapers, straws, and cups. I will set out glue and tape that you can use to hold your bridge together. You cannot use anything else to build your bridge.

The object is to build a bridge that is as strong as possible. One rule is that the bridges need to be off the ground, resting on supports. After ten minutes, I will test each bridge by placing one book at a time on it. The bridge that can hold the most books will be the winner. You may start now.

While groups are working, circulate to help groups get started. Give groups a three minute and a one minute warning before you ask them to stop working. After ten minutes, tell groups to stop.

Walk around the room and look at the bridges other groups made. Decide which bridge you think looks the strongest.

We will test each bridge by placing books on it.

Give students a few minutes to do this.

Go from bridge to bridge, placing books on each until it collapses. Note how many books the bridge held. When you have determined a winner, have everyone applaud them for their good work.

Have kids form a circle. Discuss with the students why the winning bridge won and what made it so strong.

What are some things that make a strong bridge?

(Strong building materials, good construction, good plans.)

Bridges aren't strong because they are big. Their strength depends on what they are made of and how they are built.

The Bible tells us that some people tried to build a bridge to God. It was called the Tower of Babel. These people did not succeed because no one can build a bridge or a tower to God.

Read Romans 3:23.

This verse tells us that there is a gap between God and us. We cannot reach God because we are sinners. God can't even look on sin. Sin separates us from God. We need a bridge, but is has to be so strong that it will never break or crumble.

What are some ways people try to get to God?

(By being good, going to church, not swearing or lying or stealing, being baptized, taking Communion.)

These things will never get us to God. The Bible tells us that there is only one way to get to Heaven.

Read Matthew 7:13, 14.

What do you think a small or narrow way means in this verse?

(It means that it's a hard path to go on and it isn't like a superhighway.)
Read John 14:6.

Why did Jesus say this?

(Because he died on the cross for our sins and is the only person who can get us to Heaven.)

When Jesus died on the cross, he paid for all our sin. The only way we can get to Heaven is by trusting in Jesus. All the other ways we mentioned will never fill the gap between God and us.

Distribute the crosses you made previously.

Write these words on your cross: Jesus is the only way or bridge to God.

Give students a few moments to do this.

Let's thank Jesus right now for providing a way to God.

You can use this prayer or one of your own:

Dear Jesus, thank you for being the only way to God. Thank you for bridging the gap between us and God. Thank you for dying on the cross to take away our sin. Amen.

Take your cross home and hang it in your bedroom to remind you that Jesus is the only bridge to God. Thank him every day for bridging the gap for you.

JESUS IS OUR BRIDGE TO GOD

PARENTS:

Today in class, your child learned that trusting in Jesus is the only bridge to God. The students were given paper plates, straws, cups, newspapers, tape, and glue. Using those materials, they built the strongest bridges possible. The strength of each bridge was tested by putting a load of books on it. We then discussed that people try to build bridges to get to God by going to church, doing good things, and other works. But we found out in the Bible that the only way to God is through his Son, Jesus Christ.

FAMILY FUN:

Our class discussed bridges and what made them strong. If possible, take your family to a bridge nearby and observe what makes it strong. Be sure to bring a Bible with you. If it is in a park or near a river, enjoy the nature around you. If there are no bridges available, go to the beach or lake or a sandbox and build bridges in the sand. See who in the family can build the biggest bridge. If you have winter weather and snow, you can build some bridges outside in the snow! After enjoying these activities find a place where you can sit down and read these verses in the Bible: John 14:6, Acts 2:38, Romans 10:9, Colossians 1:12-14, 1 Peter 1:4. Discuss the following questions:

How can you be saved?

What is the only way to get to the Father?

What are we to do to the Father for allowing us to share in the inheritance in Heaven?

What words describe our inheritance in Heaven? What does that mean?

Compare this to the bridges you made today or the bridge you observed. What will happen to the things we make? Will this ever happen to the bridge that gets us to the Father?

BIBLE VERSE:

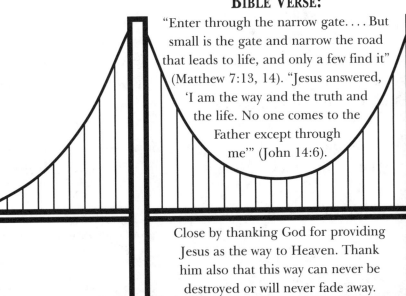

"Enter through the narrow gate. . . . But small is the gate and narrow the road that leads to life, and only a few find it" (Matthew 7:13, 14). "Jesus answered, 'I am the way and the truth and the life. No one comes to the Father except through me'" (John 14:6).

Close by thanking God for providing Jesus as the way to Heaven. Thank him also that this way can never be destroyed or will never fade away.

7
PICK IT ALL UP

ACTS 1:8

BIBLE VERSE

"You will receive power when the Holy Spirit comes on you" (Acts 1:8).

OBJECTIVE

The students will learn that Jesus gives them the power to do what's right.

MATERIALS

Bibles, copper wire, large nails, 1 1/2 volt batteries, paper clips, insulated tape or rubber, pencils, flashlight without batteries

BEFORE CLASS

Before class, construct your own electromagnet by following the instructions in this lesson. Then disassemble the magnet. Reassemble it as you give directions to the students to assemble theirs. Put labels on the batteries that say "Jesus."

In different areas of your room, set up four centers with these items in each: Bible, a piece of wire about one foot long, a large nail, two long pieces of insulator tape, scissors, about 15-20 paper clips, and paper and pencils.

When students arrive, form four groups. Assign one person to be the leader. Then have groups sit in a circle on the floor.

Who can name some powerful things here on earth?

(Spaceships, nuclear power plants, large boats, steamroller, earthquakes, tornadoes, kings or presidents.)

These things are very powerful. But there is someone who is

more powerful than any of these things or people. Who is this person?

> *(Jesus, God.)*

What are some special things that Jesus can do?

> *(Heal people, create the world, stop the wind, bring people back from the dead.)*

Did you know that we can have Jesus' power, too?

> Read Acts 1:8.

When we receive Jesus as our Savior and become part of God's family, the Holy Spirit comes to live in us. He gives us Christ's power. That doesn't mean we can do everything that Jesus did. After all, Jesus is God. But it does mean that he gives us the power to do what's right.

Let's do an activity that shows how this power works. Each group can use one work area that I have set up.

> Help groups find a work area. Direct their attention to you.

Today, we're going to make an electromagnet. We will assemble it from the items in front of you. Your leader will help you decide who does each task. Listen carefully as I give each direction.

First of all, look at the battery. I have labeled each battery with the name "Jesus." It represents Jesus and his power. Jesus is our source of power just as this battery will be the source of power in our experiment.

> Hold up the flashlight and try to turn it on.

Why do you think this flashlight doesn't work?

> *(It doesn't have any batteries.)* Open the flashlight and show them that it has no batteries.

You're right. This flashlight has no batteries. Without them, the flashlight has no source of power. It looks fine on the outside but on the inside it's empty.

Now pick up the nail and the copper wire. Take the wire and wrap it around the nail five times. Wrap the middle of the wire around the middle of nail, leaving the ends free. It is important that you only wrap the wire around the nail five times.

33

Children have a hard time following detailed directions unless they have a visual example. Show the students what to do by wrapping the wire around your nail. At each new direction, do the same. Make sure each group has wrapped their nail properly before going on.

Let's have this nail and wire represent us. Now try to see if the nail will pick up the paper clips by touching the nail to the clips.

Give groups a few moments to try this.

It was impossible to pick up those clips. This nail is like a person who doesn't know Jesus as Savior. He or she has no power to keep from doing wrong. It's hard for this person to do right, too. But when we ask Jesus to forgive our sins and ask him to live in us, we become connected to his power. To show how this works, let's connect our wires to the battery posts. Twist each end around the post and wrap it with the black tape. Tape it very securely so the wires will stay put.
  Now try to pick up some paper clips.

Give groups time to do this. Each person will want to try. Students will find this exciting so be prepared for enthusiasm.

How many paper clips will your magnet pick up?
  (Answers will vary.)

Now our nail has power. It has become an electromagnet. That is like what happens to us. When we know Jesus in a personal way, we receive power from the Holy Spirit to do what's right. We receive answers to prayer. Of course, we still do things that are wrong. Let's think about how we can get more power to do what's right. Let's find out by looking up some verses in the Bible.

Have the students come away from their work area to look up the verses listed below so the equipment doesn't distract them. Assign each group one verse to report on to the class. Give groups a few minutes to work, then have them go back to their work areas.

Let's read Romans 1:17.

Have a person from the group that was assigned this verse

read it aloud. After each question, have that same group report their answer.

What does this verse tell us helps us do what's right?
(Faith.)

Trusting Jesus will help us do what's right. Leaders, take your electromagnet and twist more wire onto the nail. We will let the extra wire represent trusting Jesus day by day.
Allow leaders time to twist wire.

Let's read 2 Timothy 3:16.
Have someone from the assigned group read the verse aloud.

What does this verse tell us helps us do what's right?
(Reading the Bible.)

Reading the Bible every day will help us do what's right. Leaders, take your electromagnet and twist more wire onto the nail. We will let that represent reading the Bible every day.
Give leaders a few moments to finish.

Let's read 2 Corinthians 13:7.
Have a volunteer from the assigned group read the verse.

What does this verse say helps us to do what's right?
(Praying.)

We increase our power to do what's right by praying every day. Leaders, take your electromagnet and twist more wire onto the nail. We will let that represent praying every day.
Give leaders a few moments to finish.

Finally, let's read Matthew 6:33.
Have a volunteer from the assigned group read the verse aloud.

What does this verse say helps us to do what's right?
(Seeking God's kingdom.)

Seeking God's kingdom means thinking about and meditating on Jesus and his example. This helps us to be more like him. Leaders, take your electromagnet and twist more wire onto the nail.

Doing all these things gives us power to do what's right. All of us know Christians who seem to be strong in their faith. It's because they are trusting Jesus, reading their Bibles and praying every day, and seeking God's kingdom.

I'm sure you probably thought the way to increase power in our battery was to get a bigger one. But we didn't need to switch our source of power to make the nail stronger. We just needed to coil more wire around it. That's what our leaders did as we read about different ways to increase our power to do what's right.

Now try picking up the paper clips.

> Give students time to try this. Their electromagnets will be able to pick up many more clips.

How many clips were you able to pick up this time?

(Answers will vary.)

We increased our power to the nail by coiling more wire around it. We increase our power to do what's right by trusting Jesus more, reading the Bible and praying every day, and seeking God's kingdom above all.

Bow your heads for a moment. Think to yourself. Do you have enough power to do what's right? If you don't, silently ask God to give you more power. Tell him the things you need to do to increase your power, like reading the Bible more often or praying more often.

> Give students a few moments to think, then close with a prayer similar to this one:

Dear Jesus, thank you for giving us the power to do what's right. Help us to read our Bibles and pray every day this week. Amen.

LIGHT IT UP

BIBLE VERSE:

"You will receive power when the Holy Spirit comes on you" (Acts 1:8).

PARENTS:

Today in class, your child learned that Jesus gives him or her power to do what is right. We made electromagnets using batteries, wire, and a nail. We compared the battery to our power source Jesus Christ. We were represented by the wire and nail. After putting our electromagnet together, we tried to pick up paper clips. We found out that if we coiled the wire more, our electromagnet would have more power. We compared this to our Christian life. When we read our Bibles, pray, use our faith, and seek God's kingdom, we gain more power to do what is right because we are closer to Jesus.

THE RIGHT LIGHTS:

Sit down with your family and talk about how Jesus wants us to do what is right. Read these verses together and discuss each one: Psalm 51:10, Psalm 119:128, Proverbs 8:6, Proverbs 12:5, Proverbs 20:11, and Proverbs 21:8. Discuss how the things we say, what we think, and how we act can help us do right. Have each family member think of some way that he or she has a hard time doing right. It could be keeping a room clean, obeying parents right away, fighting with siblings, gossiping at work, watching too much TV.

Have each person pick one thing to work on this week. Assign family members a color. When they do what is right in that area, have them color a light bulb. When the lights are all lit, discuss feelings about doing right. Talk about how Jesus helps us do right. Then take the family for a drive. It would be good to go just at twilight. Go to a place where you can see the city lights or a park that has lots of lights. Watch as the lights turn on and discuss how much power it takes to light them. Then discuss how Jesus has even more power which he has given to us.

When finished go out for ice cream or have a treat at home. As you eat, discuss Philippians 4:13. Let family members share some of the ways that Christ has helped them to have power to do what's right.

8
I'M ATTRACTED TO JESUS
JAMES 4:8

BIBLE VERSE | "Come near to God and he will come near to you" (James 4:8).

OBJECTIVE | The students will discover that we are attracted to Jesus because of his wonderful, loving characteristics.

MATERIALS | Bibles, eight plastic foam balls (you may substitute puffed wheat pieces or packing peanuts), four pieces of wool cloth, four plastic combs, four shoe boxes, tape, thread, scissors; and a red, green, blue, and yellow marker

As students arrive, mark the back of one of their hands in either a red, green, blue, or yellow stripe. When class begins, have students form groups according to the color on their hands. Give each group two foam balls, a comb, a piece of wool cloth, and a shoe box. If you have a small group, you may form two groups or even one. Have students sit in groups on the floor around you.

What kind of people do fans like to see?

(Movie stars, rock bands, pro basketball players.)

Why do these people attract so much attention?

(Because they can dunk the basketball and make thirty points a game, or because they're really good looking.)

Today we're going to talk about someone who attracts many people. Of course, that person is Jesus. Let's try an experiment that helps us understand why people are attracted to Jesus.

Set out tape, thread, and scissors. Give groups these step-by-step instructions. Don't go on to the next point until all groups have finished the one you're on.

1. Tape a foam ball to the end of a 5-inch piece of thread.
2. Tape the other end of the thread to the bottom of the shoe box.
3. Rub the comb with the wool cloth.
4. Hold up the box so that the ball hangs free.
5. Bring the comb close to the ball.

The comb will attract the ball. When all groups have tried the experiment a couple of times, have students set their equipment on the floor.

What happened to the ball when the comb came near it?

(It moved toward the comb. It was attracted to the comb.)

Read James 4:8.

How is the comb and ball experiment like what this verse describes about God?

(The ball comes near the comb when the comb comes near the ball, just like we draw near to God and he draws near to us.)

People were attracted to Jesus when he lived as a man on this earth. Think about how the disciples left their fishing nets when Jesus came near. Let's see what the crowds did.

Give paper, pencils, and one of these references to each group: Matthew 4:24, 25; Mark 3:7; Luke 6:17-19; Matthew 21:7-11.

As a group, read your Scripture. Then brainstorm reasons why people were attracted to Jesus. You can find some reasons in your verses and think up one of your own. I'll give you five minutes.

After five minutes, have each group report the reasons they wrote on their paper.

Can you think of someone in the Bible who did not follow Jesus? Who is he or she?

(Judas, the Pharisees, some rich people.)

39

Let's try something with our combs and balls to show this.

Give groups these step-by-step instructions:

1. Tape the second ball to another 5-inch piece of thread.
2. Tape the second ball next to the first one so they are touching.
3. Rub the cloth with the comb again.
4. Bring the comb near the balls.

This time the first ball should move toward the comb but the second one won't. After they have tried their experiment several times, have kids put their equipment down again.

What happened to the second ball?

(It didn't move toward the comb.)

How is this like people who don't love Jesus?

(They don't get close to Jesus. They stay by themselves away from God.)

The first ball was attracted to the comb. We are attracted to Jesus and he comes near to us.

Read John 10:27.

As child of God, we have a relationship with Jesus. He loves us. We love him. He speaks to us through the Bible. We talk to him in prayer. People who like each other spend lots of time together. They get to know each other more and more.

People who like each other say nice things about each other, too. Saying nice things about Jesus is called praising him. Right now, let's tell Jesus what we like about him.

Using sentence prayers, have volunteers praise Jesus for what they like about him.

After students have finished, close with a prayer of praise.

SECRETS, SECRETS

BIBLE VERSE:
"Come near to God and he will come near to you" (James 4:8).

PARENTS:
Today in class, your child participated in a demonstration to illustrate how people are attracted to Jesus. We rubbed a plastic comb with a piece of wool cloth, then put the comb near a plastic foam ball. The ball was attracted to the comb. We then discussed how we are drawn to Jesus because of his love for us.

FAMILY PROJECT:
As a family discuss what attracted people to Jesus. Here are some suggested Scriptures you can use:

    Loving—John 15:13
    Kind—2 Peter 1:7
    Patient—2 Peter 3:9
    Forgiving—Luke 23:34
    Helping—Hebrews 13:6
    Faithful—Hebrews 10:33

Then discuss how people are attracted to us when we act like Jesus. For the next week, have each person do one of the characteristics you discussed for someone in the family—but do it secretly. The following are examples:

Take out the trash when Mother isn't looking.
Put an I-Love-You note on someone's pillow.
Make someone's favorite snack and put it in his or her bedroom.
Quietly let someone else go first in the bathroom when getting ready for school.

At the end of the week, treat the family to a night out. Before leaving, have each person reveal the nice things he or she secretly did for other family members.

9
GREAT GIFTS
ROMANS 12:6

BIBLE VERSE

"We have different gifts, according to the grace given us" (Romans 12:6).

OBJECTIVE

Students will learn that they can trust God to give them a gift to use in the body of Christ.

MATERIALS

Bible, items listed on the chart, a picture, a bell, spray perfume bottle, cotton ball, cookie broken into small pieces, pencils, and a copy of the "Sense"ible Test sheet at the end of this lesson for each student

Although this lesson requires a number of items, kids love to hear, smell, taste, touch, and look at things. Most of the required items are ones you can find in your kitchen.

BEFORE CLASS

Before class, put together the following items to make different stations in your classroom. Set up the stations by placing the items in separate areas and putting a label on each station such as Station 1, Station 2, and so forth.

You can do this lesson by setting up centers or if you have a small class, do it as one group activity. If you have more than ten students in your class, centers are a must. Ask three or four helpers to manage the stations. If you have responsible older students, you may ask them to help at the stations. Brief your helpers on how to let the students test their sense. At Stations 1, 2, 3, and 4, the students should not look at the items.

To set up the centers, put station items at different tables or areas. Label each station with the appropriate number by writing it on a piece of paper and setting it near the items. Assign helpers to each station and explain what will happen at each. If you have only two helpers, assign them to Stations 1 and 4.

When students arrive, have them sit in a circle. Set the picture, bell, perfume, cotton ball, and cookie pieces within reach.

STATION	ITEMS NEEDED	STATION SET-UP
1: hearing	celery, crisp potato chips, canned whipping cream, raw spaghetti	Place all items in the paper bag and write a number 1 on the bag.
2: smell	cinnamon, garlic powder, dry coffee grounds	Seal envelopes and consecutively mark them with numbers 1, 2, and 3.
3: taste	syrup, dill pickle juice, salt, cocoa, cotton swabs	Put each ingredient in a separate covered container and label the containers with numbers 1 through 4. Set the cotton swabs near the containers.
4: touch	paper bag, one soft, one hard, one rough, and one smooth item. (You might use a tissue, a hard ball, a piece of sandpaper, and a pencil.)	Place all items in the bag and mark the bag with number 4.
5: sight	ten items of various sizes and colors, tray, towel	Put items on the tray and cover with a towel.

God has given us five senses to help us know what is happening around us.

When you are at home and someone is at your door to visit, how do you know they are there?

> *(They knock or ring the doorbell.)*
> Ring the bell.

When we hear this sound, we know it is a bell. This is one of our senses called hearing.

What kinds of things do you hear every day?

> *(My dog barks a lot. My baby sister cries every night.)*
> Hold up the picture.

43

What sense do we use to appreciate this picture?
> *(Sight.)*

What are some of your favorite things to see?
> *(A pizza, myself in new clothes, baseball cards.)*
> Spray the perfume.

Now what sense are we using?
> *(Smell.)*

What's one of your favorite smells?
> *(Popcorn, flowers.)*
> Pass around the cotton ball.

What sense are you using when you hold the cotton ball?
> *(Touch.)*

What things do you like to touch?
> *(Bubble bath bubbles, my mom's soft hair.)*
> Pass around the cookie pieces.

Take a piece and eat it. What sense are we using now?
> *(Taste.)*

What's your favorite taste?
> *(Chocolate, peanut butter, fizzy soda.)*

We have just used all five of our senses. Today, you will get a chance to test your senses. As you test each one, try to decide which one is your best sense.
> Distribute "Sense"ible Test sheets and pencils.
> Form five groups. If you have younger students, make sure they are in a group with older students and assign the older students to help them. Point out each center.

At Station 1, you will test your hearing. At Station 2, you will test your sense of smell. At Station 3, you will test your taste buds. At Station 4, you will test your sense of touch. And at Station 5, you will test your sight. Each Station is marked by its number. Follow the directions on your "Sense"ible Test sheet for that station. When I ring the bell, move to the next station on your right.

Assign each group a specific center to start on. Have them pass from one station to the next consecutively. Watch to see when groups finish testing their sense, then ring the bell. Usually 3 to 5 minutes will be enough time. Ring the bell one more time when everyone has finished their "Sense"ible Test sheets.

Then hold up the items at each station and reveal the right answers. Have students check their answers on their test sheets as you give the answers.

If you are doing this test as a whole class, use these directions:

1. Go to the back of the room where students cannot see you and break each food item. Give students time to write down their answers after each sound. Reveal and discuss the sound after everyone has finished writing.

2. Take the envelopes around from student to student and let each person smell each scent. When students have completed writing their answers, identify the scents.

3. Let each student taste the food in each container. Be sure to use a new swab with each taste. Allow time for students to write their answers. Then reveal what the foods are.

4. Call students up one at a time and let them feel inside the bag. Then have them go back to their seats and write down the four things they felt in the bag. When all have finished, hold up the items and let students see if their answers are right or wrong.

5. Unveil the tray for thirty seconds while students stare at the ten items. Then cover the tray and have them write down the names of as many items as they can remember. When they finish, remove the towel and let the students check their answers.

Which one of your five senses did you get the most right answers with?

(Allow students to share.)

Just as you have one or two senses that are better than the others, you also have other talents that are outstanding. The Bible tells us that God has given each of us different talents or gifts to use in the church. Just like our five senses, each person has a strong gift.

Read Romans 12:6.

What are some of the talents that God has given to people in our church?

(Singing, preaching, teaching, helping others, caring for little children.)

God has given each of us at least one special gift. Our minister's gift is preaching. Our church needs his gift. Other people in our church can sing well. Our church needs their gifts. Some people like to help others. That is also a very important gift. And still others can teach well. Our church needs all the gifts that God has given us.

Share one or two of the gifts God has given you. Also mention gifts of people who may not have high profiles in your church, like the janitor, the person who drives the church bus, or the team that prepares food for church functions. Then allow students to share some things that they do well in the church or in helping others. Be sure to affirm the gifts of students who are too shy to mention any or others who may not feel like they have a gift.

As you grow older, you will find more strong gifts that you can use in the church. But even at your age, you have talents and gifts that God can use. You could ask others to come to church with you. You can listen quietly when God's Word is taught. You could cheer up people who are sick or who can't come to church because they are too old.

Right now, let's thank God for the gifts he has given the people in our church.

Have volunteers thank God for different people and their gifts in the church.

Now think about something you can do to honor God in the church. It may be something you've never done before or something you do often. Silently ask God to help you do this sometime before our next meeting.

Allow students time to pray. Then close with a prayer similar to this one:

Dear heavenly Father, thank you for giving each of us special gifts to use in your church. Help us to use them often. In Jesus' name, amen.

This week, whenever you use one of your five senses, thank God for the special gifts he has given to his people in the church.

GREAT GIFTS

BIBLE VERSE:

"We have different gifts, according to the grace given us" (Romans 12:6).

PARENTS:

Today in class, your child learned that he or she can trust God to give him or her a gift to use in church. They tested their five senses by listening to different foods, smelling different spices, tasting sweet and sour foods, feeling different textures, and looking at ten different items and recalling what they saw. We then discussed which of our five senses was the strongest. We related this to the church, which is the body of Christ. We discussed how all of us have different strong gifts in the church body. We thanked God for those people in our church who are using their gifts and thought about ways we could help our church body.

LET'S TRY OUR FIVE SENSES:

Each night this week have some fun during family time. Try different tests with your five senses. You can use the ideas below or make up your own. When finished with each trial, read the Bible verse that talks about that sense and discuss the questions.

•**Monday—Hearing Night**—Have each family member find something in the house that makes a sound and bring it to family time. Make sure the item is concealed so that no one knows what it is. While everybody's eyes are closed, let each person make their sound to see who can guess what it is. (Romans 10:17) What are ways that we can hear the Word of God to increase our faith?

•**Tuesday—Tasting Night**—Follow Monday night's directions, but have each person bring a favorite food to taste. (James 3:5 and Philippians 2:11) What are some things that we do with our tongues that God does not like? What are some things we can do with our tongues that God does like?

•**Wednesday—Smelling Night**—Follow Monday night's directions, but have each person bring a favorite smell to share, such as a food, perfume, or flower. (Philippians 4:18) Paul talks about a gift here that people sent him and refers to it as a fragrant aroma. Talk about different things we can do for others that would be like a sweet aroma to them.

•**Thursday—Sight Night**—Bring a blanket and some common everyday items. Have two people hold up a blanket in front of a table or chair and place an item on the chair or table. When he or she drops the blanket, see who can identify the item the fastest. (1 Peter 3:4) What is precious in the sight of God in this verse? Name other things that are precious in his sight.

•**Friday—Feeling Night**—Bring in a bag with different items and see if all items can be identified just by touch. (1 John 5:18) God keeps Satan from touching us. What does this mean?

"Sense"ible Test

Station 1: Hearing

Listen as each food is broken behind you. Guess what food it is and record your answer.

1.
2.
3.
4.

Station 2: Smell

Gently sniff each envelope without looking at the contents. Write down what you think the scent is.

1.
2.
3.
4.

Station 3: Taste

Taste each food by dabbing the end of a clean cotton swab into it and putting the food on your tongue. Use each swab only once. Write down what you think the food is.

1.
2.
3.
4.

Station 4: Touch

Reach in the bag and feel the items. Write down what you think each item is.

1.
2.
3.
4.

Station 5: Sight

When the tray is uncovered, you will have thirty seconds to look at the items. Then write down as many as you can remember.

10
ALL FOR ONE, ONE FOR ALL

1 CORINTHIANS 12:13

BIBLE VERSE | "We were all baptized by one Spirit into one body" (1 Corinthians 12:13).

OBJECTIVE | The students will learn that they can trust God to make us all part of one family.

MATERIALS | Bible, blindfolds, pencils, two coloring pictures for each child, crayons, several extra pairs of shoes with laces, newspapers

BEFORE CLASS | Before class, acquire two pictures to color for each student from a coloring book. The pictures do not necessarily have to be the same for all students. Set pictures out in pairs on work areas. Cover work areas with newspapers to avoid getting crayon marks on the surface. Set out six crayons and a blindfold beside each set of pictures.

When students arrive, ask them to sit in a circle.

Today, we're going to talk about our bodies and try some activities with our arms and legs and eyes.

Give students time to try each of the following activities:

Stand and touch your toes. Jump as high as you can.
Sit down and try to touch your toe to your nose.

Not everyone will be able to do this, but have kids see how close they can get.

49

Our bodies are amazing. Think of all the things you did.
    What parts of your body did you use to touch your toe to your nose?

                       (Almost every part of my body.)

What parts of your body did you use when you jumped as high as you could?

                       (Arms, knees, feet.)

What would happen if your arm said, "It's my day off. I'm not going to do anything"? Or what if one of your legs said, "I quit." Now you can't use that leg. To illustrate how hard it is to do things without all the parts of your body, try to stand up and touch your toes using only one leg.

            Allow students to try this. They should find it almost impossible to do.

That was very hard to do. Please sit down again. Now let's pretend that your mouth says, "I'm tired so I'm staying closed." Try to take a deep breath with your mouth closed.

            Give kids a moment to do this.

You couldn't take a very deep breath with your mouth closed. That's because your mouth and nose work together.

            Have students form pairs. If you have younger students, pair them with older ones.

You and your partner will work together for this activity. I have set out pictures for each pair. Please find a set a pictures that you can use.

            Direct pairs to sets of pictures.

I want you to color this picture—blindfolded. This is how we will do it. Choose which partner will go first. Then put the blindfold on that partner. When you are blindfolded, make sure that you can't see anything. Your partner is not allowed to say anything to you once you can't see.
    Now find a crayon and color your picture. Do the best job you can.

            Give blindfolded partners 3-5 minutes to color. Call time and have them take off their blindfolds and look at what they've done. Then have pairs blindfold the other partner and repeat the activity. Be prepared for giggles and laughter. When the second partner has colored for 3-5 minutes, stop the activity.

We have some funny pictures. Coloring is hard to do without your eyes. Now we will try blindfolded coloring again. This time, your partner can tell you what color to choose and he or she can guide your hands so you get in the right place. Let's see what a difference this makes.

Again give students 3-5 minutes to color, blindfolded with guidance. Then have partners change roles and do the activity again. When the second set of partners has finished, continue.

Let's sit back in our circle. Bring your pictures with you and sit beside your partner.

Once students have settled into the circle, have each person hold up his or her pictures and have other students guess which one was done with and without a partner's help. Praise the pictures in which the partners worked together. When everyone has had a chance to display their work, continue.

It was hard to color with your eyes covered.
 How did you feel when you worked on the picture without any help?

(Frustrated. I knew my picture wasn't going to be any good. I wanted to use my eyes. I felt confused about where the picture was.)

Looking at your pictures, I can see that you did a better job with help. How did you feel when you had a partner guiding you?

(Happy. I was glad he could tell me what to do. I knew my picture would be better.)

The second time, you depended on your partner to help. You needed him or her to tell you which color to pick and where to color. That's the way the parts of our body depend on each other. Your hand can't color the picture by itself. It needs your brains and your eyes. Let's try one more activity to see how the parts of our bodies depend on each other to get things done. We will try to tie our shoes with one hand. If you don't have tie shoes, raise your hand. I have a shoe you can use.

51

Take out the extra shoes you brought and distribute one to each person who doesn't have shoes with laces. Have kids put one hand behind their back. Then give students about five minutes to try to tie one shoe. This activity is impossible without two hands.

I'm sure no one could tie his or her shoes with one hand. Now turn to your partner, and each of you use one hand to tie one pair of shoelaces. You can help each other. For example, each of you could hold one lace.

Give kids about five minutes to try tying their shoes this way.

Working together makes it easier to tie shoelaces. That's because you depended on your partner's help. Without your partner, you couldn't tie the shoelaces.

This is how the parts of our body depend on each other. We do many things every day that we couldn't do without two hands or two feet or two eyes, such as climbing a tree, jumping rope, or swimming. God's Word talks about a different kind of body.

Read 1 Corinthians 12:13.

This verse is talking about the worldwide church. The Bible calls all Christians the body of Christ. Everyone who has accepted Jesus as their Savior is part of the body of Christ. What is the most important part of your body?

(Head.)

Who do you think is the most important person and the head of the body of Christ?

(Jesus.)

Let's look in our Bibles to see who is the head.

Let a volunteer read Colossians 1:18.

In a physical body, what does the head do for the other parts?

(Tells them what to do. Thinks for the rest of the body.)

Just as your head controls every part of your body, Christ controls the church. We are his hands, his feet, his eyes, his

mouth on earth. But we need to ask him to guide us in whatever we do. Let's look at how the body works together.

Have a volunteer read Ephesians 4:16.

In this verse, it says that the body of Christ fits together perfectly. Each individual part needs to work together to make the body grow. Just as your body grows, the church grows to be more mature and healthy.

Reread the end of the verse.

What are we trying to build up the church to do?

(Have love and love each other.)

Remember that we said each part of our bodies has a different job to do? How does the same thing work in the body of Christ? (We all do different things in the church. Everyone has a different job to do.)

Just as the parts of our body work together, so do the Christians in the body of Christ. We all depend on each other. If one person isn't doing his or her job, the body suffers. Let's thank Jesus for making us part of his family or body.

You can use the following prayer or one of your own:

Dear heavenly Father, thank you for including us in the body of Christ. Help us do the job you want us to do. Help us love each other as members of his family. In Jesus' name, amen.

This week when you are writing, coloring, jumping, or doing other fun things with your body, think about how God made us part of his body, the church, and how we depend on others to help Christ's body grow and become healthy.

BODY BUILD-UP

BIBLE VERSE:

"We were all baptized by one spirit into one body" (1 Corinthians 12:13).

PARENTS:

Today in class, your child learned that we can trust God to make us all part of one body or family—Christ's church. We found out that our bodies can do amazing things when each part works together. To illustrate this, your child tried to color a picture without using his or her eyes. It was much easier to do when a partner helped by being "the eyes." Your child also tried to tie a shoe with just one arm. It was impossible. Again it was much easier with a partner who could also use only one arm. We compared this to Christ's body, the church. We discussed how we all need to work together to build up the body of Christ because we are all part of one body.

FAMILY EXERCISE:

For the next two weeks, do an exercise regimen every night with your family. It can be as simple as jumping jacks or running in place. You could jog or ride bikes every day. The first day, write down how many repetitions each person did or how far he or she could go. Do the exercises for two weeks. Increase repetitions or distance as you build up your stamina. After two weeks get together and discuss the following questions:

How does your body feel differently
    now than it did two weeks ago?
What was the hardest thing
    about exercising?
What was the nicest thing
    about exercising?

Then discuss what the Bible says about Christ's body, the church. Read 1 Corinthians 12:12-27. Discuss these questions:

Are some members of the body of Christ more important than others? (Verses 14-18)
How should the members treat one another? (Verse 25)
What are some ways we can show this? (Read Ephesians 4:12-16.)
As members of the body of Christ, what are we supposed to do? (Verse 12)
What are some ways we can build up the body of Christ? (Verses 13-15)
What causes the body of Christ to grow? (Verse 16)

For the next two weeks, work as a family to build up the body of Christ, the church. You could work in the nursery together, help in children's church, do service work around the church building, etc. After two weeks, get together and discuss the same questions you asked after two weeks of exercising your bodies. This time apply the principles of body building to the church.

11
IT HURTS!
1 CORINTHIANS 12:26

BIBLE VERSE

"If one part [of the body of Christ] suffers, every part suffers with it; if one part is honored, every part rejoices with it" (1 Corinthians 12:26).

OBJECTIVE

The students will discover that what happens to one person in the body of Christ affects all the others. With God's help and our trust in him, we can help each other.

MATERIALS

Bibles, rolled bandages (adding machine paper may be substituted), adhesive tape, party hats, cake or cupcakes, beverage, napkins, watch with a second hand

BEFORE CLASS

Remove furniture from the middle of the room to allow space for a relay race. You may also do this activity in a fellowship hall or gym. Clearly mark the beginning of the race, then mark the end of the race about fourteen feet away. You may either mark lines with tape or if your room is small enough, have the relay teams touch the wall and come back to the starting line.

As students arrive, assign them numbers from one to four. Send each group to a different corner of the room. Continue when students have formed teams in their separate corners.

Choose two volunteers on your team to act as an injured person.

After students have chosen two people, give two rolled

bandages to each team. If your groups are large enough, you may divide the teams in half and let each half help one injured player.

Your injured person has just fallen down the stairs. Now he has a broken leg. Help him by bandaging his leg. He's really hurting, so be careful.

Give kids a few moments to bandage the legs.

Now we have to get our injured people to the hospital. But all the ambulances in town are out on calls. So the rest of you will have to act as emergency squads. We will start the race with two teams. The two teams will line up with their first injured person. The second injured person will wait on the sidelines until the others come back and cross the line and tag the new emergency team. Then the team will help the second injured person go to the far line and back again. When both of your injured team members have gone to the far line and come back to cross the finish line, you are done with your race.

Select the two teams to start, and have them line up at the starting line with their first injured person.

Emergency squads, your injured person is in so much pain that he or she can't step on his or her foot. You must help him or her hop to the other mark I have put on the floor, then back again. Then you must help your second injured person do the same. The team who crosses the finish line first has the best emergency team. I will time each team to determine the winner. Are the first two teams ready? Okay, ready, set, go!

Time the two teams that race first. Then have the other two teams line up and time them while they race. When all kids have crossed the finish line, have the students remove the bandages. Set them aside so they won't distract your class. Announce the winning team.

Those of you who pretended to be injured, how did it feel to need help to get around?

(Frustrating. I just wanted to run by myself. It was kind of fun.)

Those of you who were on the emergency squad, what was it like to have to help someone who couldn't run well?

(I like feeling needed. He was so heavy.)

As Christians, we are all part of what the Bible calls the body of Christ. It's like your own body, which has many parts like hands, feet, eyes, nose, and ears. Yet each part is still part of your body. Being a member of Christ's body means that we are all part of one group. Let's read what happens if someone in the body of Christ gets hurt.

Read 1 Corinthians 12:26.

According to this verse, what happens when one Christian gets hurt?

(Everyone suffers and feels the hurt.)

What kind of hurts do you think this verse is talking about?

(Hurts to our body or our feelings.)

Sometimes we can hurt in our spirits, too. If we are tempted to do something wrong, if someone makes fun of us because we love Jesus, we feel hurt inside. Those kinds of hurts are harder to explain to another person. It's easy to see a hurt to our body because it bleeds or bruises. But hurts to our feelings and spirits are harder to see.

Think of a time when you were hurt in your feelings or your spirit. What happened?

How can these kinds of hurts affect you?

(I might get crabby or feel bad about myself.) Read 1 Corinthians 12:25.

If something bad happens, like you break your arm or stub your toe, how does the rest of your body feel?

(It feels bad too and tries to help the hurt part.)

As a team, all of you acted together. You acted like one part to finish the race.

How did your emergency squad help the injured person finish the race?

(We put a bandage on the person's broken leg and helped her hop. We all did our part.)

We learned that we're all part of one body or team in the Lord. Then how should we treat another Christian who is hurting?

(We should help him as much as we can. We should care about that person.)

The second part of the first verse we read tells what we should do if something good happens to someone in the body of Christ.

Reread 1 Corinthians 12:26.

What should we do for a person who has something good happen in his life?

(We should be happy with him or her and rejoice.)

It seems like it should be easy to rejoice when something good happens to someone else, but sometimes jealousy gets in the way. If a friend gets a new bike, we wish we had one, too. If your brother is praised for something he does, you feel left out. Sometimes it's harder to feel good with someone who is happy than it is to help someone who is hurting.

But it's important to rejoice with each other. Another way the Bible describes being part of Christ's body is that we are all part of God's family. Our church is one part of God's family. When we rejoice together, it makes us closer to each other in God's family. To help us feel like a family, let's practice rejoicing with each other.

Bring out the party hats, cake, and beverage.

Let's have a "surprise" birthday party. The surprise is that we're going to celebrate your birthday right now even though it may not come for months. We're just going to celebrate the fact that you were born and that you are now part of our church family.

Distribute the party hats and napkins. Have kids sit at a table. Then celebrate the "surprise" birthday for each person in your class. To do so, have each student stand while you say as a group, "We're so glad that you're here." When you finish celebrating each person, pray for the food and enjoy the snack.

BRANCHING OUT

BIBLE VERSE:

"If one part (of the body of Christ) suffers, every part suffers with it; if one part is honored, every part rejoices with it" (1 Corinthians 12:26).

PARENTS:

In class today, your child learned how we are related to each other as Christians, and that we are all part of the body of Christ. We also found out that God calls us part of his family. As Christians, we hurt when one of us hurts and rejoice when one of us rejoices. We learned this by having a relay race with one person pretending to be injured. Then we had a "surprise" birthday party when we pretended to celebrate everyone's birthday. Then we made a rejoicing circle and celebrated each person's part in the body of Christ.

To help your children understand the importance of being part of a family, make a family tree using the following diagram. You can expand it to include aunts, uncles, and cousins. Then spend time thanking God for your family and each person in it.

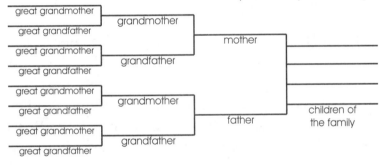

Next, make a church family tree. After you have filled in the lines as completely as possible, thank God for your church family and each person in it. Also ask God to help you recognize the needs of people in both your own family and your church family. Think of practical ways you could help others in your family and at church.

our pastor

church leaders

the families in our church

12
LET'S DO IT TOGETHER!

EPHESIANS 4:16

BIBLE VERSE | "From him the whole body, joined and held together by every supporting ligament, grows and builds itself up in love, as each part does its work" (Ephesians 4:16).

OBJECTIVE | Students will discover that as part of the body of Christ, they can work together to accomplish God's work.

MATERIALS | Bible, about 50 lunch-size paper bags, old newspapers, masking tape, markers

BEFORE CLASS | Make paper bricks by stuffing two sheets of newspaper into each lunch-size paper bag. Tape the bag closed with a gift wrapping fold so that the paper bag brick has a rectangular shape. Then shape each brick slightly so the edges look square. Make enough bricks so that your students can build a fort, house, bridge, or other building with them. If you have a lot of older students in your class, you could let them make some of the paper bag bricks while working on their building project.

Today, we're going to work together to make a large project.
> Point out the paper bricks you made earlier.

These are your building bricks. I'll give you masking tape to help you keep your project together.
First, I want you to select a construction superintendent.

He or she is the person who will direct your project. You
must listen to his or her directions.

Then, I want you all to agree on what you will build. You
could make a fort, a bridge, a building, or a wall. When you
have decided on your project, you can start. I will give you
fifteen minutes to complete your project.

> Help your class decide on a reasonable building they can
> erect. Then allow them to start. While kids are working,
> remind them to listen to the construction superintendent. This
> will be important for your discussion later.
>
> Give kids up to fifteen minutes to complete their project.
> Then admire what they made. Be sure to point out the good
> things about their work.
>
> Ask the kids to sit in a semicircle around you, but be sure
> you sit away from the project so they won't be distracted.

**It's fun to work together. As a class, we can get more done
and help each other by cooperating.
What did you like best about working together?**

> *(I didn't have to do everything by myself, I had help. I like talking to
> people when I work.)*

What was hard about working together?

> *(Someone kept taking my spot, and I didn't get enough bricks.)*

**Was it helpful or unhelpful to have a construction superin-
tendent direct your work? Why?**

> *(Helpful, because she spread out the work. Unhelpful, because he was
> too bossy.)*

**The Bible says that working together is important in the
family of God, too.**

> Read Ephesians 4:16.

**According to this verse, what happens when the body of
Christ works together?**

> *(All the parts help each other. The whole body is healthy and grows.)*

**This verse says that the way we work together best is by
becoming more and more like Jesus.
What are some good qualities that Jesus has?**

> *(He's kind. He loves people. He cares about everyone.)*

What can you do to be like Jesus in these areas?

> *(I can be kind to new kids at church. I can love people who are mean to me.)*

When we worked on our project, we had a construction superintendent who directed our work. He or she saw to it that everyone was working where they fit best.

    According to our verse, who directs the work in the body of Christ?

> *(Jesus.)*

What makes him such a good director?

> *(He knows everything. He doesn't make mistakes. He loves us so much. He's God.)*

What might happen if we don't listen to our director, Jesus?

> *(We won't do what he wants us to do. Our part of the work won't get done.)*

Unlike the project we did in class, Jesus directs the work of his kingdom and the results are perfect. Even though some of his students don't do a good job with the work he has for them, God promises that the job of the church will get done.

Read Hebrews 10:35, 36.

God promises a reward for those who work hard for his kingdom. Sometimes we get this reward here on earth. What are some rewards you have gotten recently for doing what's right?

> *(Happiness. My mom gave me a treat yesterday because I was so nice to my little sister. My little brother hugged me when I read him a book.)*

Doing what's right brings rewards right away. These rewards could be feeling good about ourselves, making others happy, or getting praise. Of course, when we get to Heaven, God will give us more rewards for how we helped work in his family.

    To help us work hard for Jesus, let's decorate a brick.

> Have kids get one brick each. Distribute one marker to each student.

Think of one talent you have that you can use for Jesus.

Perhaps you can sing well or you like to help little kids. Or maybe you can help clean up at church or encourage someone who's sad. On your brick, draw a picture of what you can do for Jesus. Give kids a few minutes to draw. Be sure you decorate a brick, too.

Let's dedicate our work to Jesus. We know that it takes all of us working together to make the body of Christ healthy. So let's build a little pile of talents for Jesus.

I'll pray and tell Jesus that we want to use our talents for him. Then I'll pause. If you want to promise to use your talent for Jesus, quietly put your brick in the center of our circle. When everyone has had a chance to place their brick, I'll close my prayer.

This is a suggested prayer you might use:

Dear heavenly Father, we have a lot of talents that you have given us. We want to use our talents for you.

Pause and place your brick in the middle of the circle. Then give kids time to place their bricks. As soon as everyone is seated again, resume your prayer.

Thank you for letting us be a part of your family. In Jesus' name, amen.

After you finish praying, have kids get their own bricks.

Take your brick home and put it where it can remind you to use your talent for Jesus.

LOVE BRICKS

BIBLE VERSE:

"From him the whole body, joined and held together by every supporting ligament, grows and builds itself up in love, as each part does its work" (Ephesians 4:16).

PARENTS:

Today in class, your child learned that we should all work together in the body of Christ. To illustrate this, we worked together as a class to make a project out of paper bag bricks. Then we discussed that Jesus is our leader who helps us build God's kingdom.

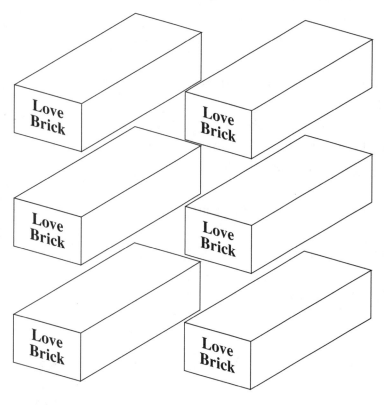

FAMILY BUILDING:

One part of helping God's family, which the Bible calls the body of Christ, is to grow strong and healthy and build each other up in love. This week, see if you can cover your refrigerator with Love Bricks. Trace or photocopy the bricks on this page. Make enough so that each person can have at least ten. Put the bricks, a pencil, and tape in a basket or bowl and set it on a counter near the refrigerator. Gather your family and read Romans 14:19. Discuss how we can build each other up in love.

Explain that each time someone does something kind or loving, he or she should write or draw the good deed on a brick and tape it to the refrigerator. See how many bricks you can tape to the refrigerator in a week. Then meet as a family and read all the kindnesses your family has done to build each other up.